A Shepherd's Care for His Sheep

A Study of Psalm 23

by Joseph Preston

A Shepherd's Care for His Sheep: A Study of Psalm 23

ISBN: 978-1-105-50124-1

 Requests for information should be addressed to Joseph Preston at WLD Ranch, 7351 Woolsey Rd. Girard, PA 16417.

Much of this material originally appeared on the WLD Ranch website in 2009 and 2010 as part of the series Knowing Life: Devotions for Knowing Jesus. Explore the current devotions at www.wldranch.com.

Photos on cover and title page by Joseph Preston

Psalm 23

A Psalm of David.
The LORD is my shepherd,
I shall not be in want.
He makes me lie down in green pastures,
he leads me beside quiet waters,
he restores my soul.
He guides me in paths of righteousness
for his name's sake.
Even though I walk through
the valley of the shadow of death,
I will fear no evil,
for you are with me;
your rod and your staff, they comfort me.
You prepare a table before me
in the presence of my enemies.
You anoint my head with oil;
my cup overflows.
Surely goodness and love will follow me
all the days of my life,
and I will dwell
in the house of the LORD
forever.

in memory of Sharon Haag,

one who knew the joy of

walking close to the Good Shepherd

in this life,

and now hears His voice

face to face

". . . and his sheep follow him because

they know his voice." (John 10:4)

dedicated to all who look for hope

despite their circumstances,

especially to those who are

learning to trust the Good Shepherd

during their battle with cancer

Contents

Introduction

Psalm 23 is one of the most commonly quoted passages of Scripture and it is one of the first Bible passages many of us ever learned. Because of its familiarity, sometimes we can get too comfortable and think that we've gotten *beyond* "the 23rd Psalm" in our Christian life. But let's examine the 23rd Psalm once again.

Psalm 23 has encouraged many people in the approximately three thousand years since it was written by David. Its poetic and vivid words have a way of bringing comfort to people in difficult circumstances. It also has a way of urging people toward a deeper, trust-based intimacy with God.

This study will encourage you to walk close to the Shepherd of Psalm 23. As you read these pages, I want to challenge you to look for hope despite your circumstances. Learn to trust the Good Shepherd no matter what life may bring.

The Shepherd's Name

Psalm 23 begins by identifying who the psalm is about: "The LORD is my shepherd." Our generic English word "Lord" doesn't quite communicate all that David meant to communicate when he wrote the first words of this psalm. Notice in most translations the practice of using small capitals to indicate that this is a translation of the word "Yahweh." This is not just a title such as we think of when we use the word "lord" – "my lord," "Lord Henry," or even "Lord Jesus." Each of these uses the word "Lord" as a title, not a personal name.

But Psalm 23 starts with the same word used in Exodus 3 when Moses asked God "If they ask me for your name, what do I tell them?" (a paraphrase of Exodus 3:13). God's answer is that "I AM WHO I AM. This is what you are to say to the Israelites: 'I AM has sent me to you' . . . 'The LORD [Yahweh], the God of your fathers – the God of Abraham, the God of Isaac and the God of Jacob – has sent me to you.' This is my name forever, the name by which I am to be remembered from generation to generation" (Exodus 3:14-15 NIV). The word "Yahweh" comes from the word for "I am." This is God's self-identifying name. He wanted to be known as "I AM."

But what does God's self-designation indicate about him? Some would emphasize that the name focuses on God's self-existence, the fact of his being or existing apart from needing something else to cause his existence. He just IS. Others would emphasize that this is God's covenant name, the name he uses to establish his promises to his people. So it emphasizes his faithfulness. In reading Exodus 3:13-15, both of these areas of emphasis can be seen. "I AM WHO I AM" and "I AM has sent me to you" are odd ways of naming himself unless God really just "IS."

The reality that he exists without resulting from something else sets God apart from everything else that is derived from or results from other causes (namely, God creating all things – Genesis 1:1; Colossians 1:15-17). His existence is not to be questioned. But his faithfulness is also not to be questioned. If God has promised something, he will be faithful to carry out his promise. This can be seen when God says he is the God of their fathers and that this is how he should be remembered throughout the generations. Knowing their own history, the Israelites would know that God had been faithful to their forefathers. Based on the past, his faithfulness in the future should not be questioned. The One-Who-Is IS faithful, regardless of the time, situation, or generation.

But I'd like to mention another aspect regarding God's self-identification. Not only is "Yahweh/ Lord" God's name that indicates his self-existence and faithfulness, but it is also his name that indicates his relationship to his people. When Moses was considering God's call for him to deliver the people of Israel from Egypt, Moses knew that the people would want to know who was sending Moses to deliver them (Exodus 3:13). If the "god" Moses was following was not the true God, the God their ancestors had followed, then how could they trust this god? How would they know if this god that Moses met in the desert was really capable of freeing them from Egypt and the gods of Egypt? God's answer was to remind them of his relationship with their ancestors. God told Moses to tell the people of Israel, "The LORD [Yahweh], the God of your fathers – the God of Abraham, the God of Isaac and the God of Jacob

– has sent me to you" (Exodus 3:15). This God was not just some idol that could be worshiped along with the Egyptian gods. He was the very God who knew their ancestors personally. And he wanted to be known by future generations as the same, self-existent, faithful God. "Yahweh" is God's personal name, the name by which he wanted to be remembered, the name which speaks to his existence, his faithfulness, and his personal knowableness.

So David begins Psalm 23, "The LORD [Yahweh – the I AM] is my shepherd." David is not just speaking of his superior, his master-lord. He is speaking of the God who can be known, the God who IS, who is faithful, who is knowable. He is speaking of God with whom he has a personal relationship. A shepherd doesn't just control his sheep (be a master of the sheep). A shepherd knows his sheep and his sheep know him (John 10). And that is what David is saying. The psalm is about a relationship between shepherd and sheep, between the true God and his people.

God exists. God is faithful. God is knowable. David writes that this self-existing, faithful, knowable God is his shepherd. Just as a sheep knows and follows his shepherd, David knows and follows God as his shepherd. "The I AM is my shepherd" (Psalm 23:1, my translation). And we know and follow God in Jesus (John 1:14, 18), who tells us, "***I am*** the good shepherd; I know my sheep and my sheep know me" (John 10:14, emphasis added). Is Jesus claiming to be the subject of Psalm 23? Let's consider this next.

The Shepherd's Identity

Jesus often made statements using the words "I am" to introduce something about himself (John 6:35, 8:12, 10:11, 11:25, 14:6). In John 8:58, Jesus says, "Before Abraham was born, I am!" Jesus claims the name that God claimed for himself. All three aspects of the name "Yahweh" apply to Jesus as well.

Self-existent (no one brought him into existence):
John 1:3 says, "Through him [through Jesus] all things were made; without him nothing was made that has been made." In John 8:58, Jesus claims to be in existence before Abraham was born. This is not a normal human existence. Jesus is declaring that his existence is of a different nature than other people. In John 1:3, the Gospel writer proclaims that everything came into existence through God the Son ("the Word" in John 1:1), the one who became human through the supernatural conception and birth of Jesus (John 1:14; Matthew 1:18-25). All of creation owes its existence to the self-existent one, who himself entered his own creation by becoming a man, Jesus.

Faithful (he keeps his promises):

Jesus says, "I am with you always, to the very end of the age" (Matt. 28:20). It is not just that Jesus makes promises, because many people can make promises and faithfully keep their promises. It is the nature of the promises that Jesus makes that set him apart. He promises many things, things like eternal life, a relationship with God, forgiveness of sins, an eternal home with God (John 5:24; Mark 2:8-12; John 14:1-6; etc.).

Anyone can make grand promises, but how do we know that they will keep their promises? Jesus' promise in Matthew 28:20 demonstrates why he would be able to keep all of his promises for eternity: "I am with you always." He can keep his promises, many of them having to do with eternity, since he will be with us for eternity. And how do we know this promise is true? He gives this promise after predicting his own death and return to life, and AFTER having died on the cross and having come back to life! These are not just grandiose promises of someone who really can't keep his promises. The one who has power to die and rise back to life on his own authority (John 10:18) certainly will be able to keep all his promises.

Knowable (he is personal and wants to know us): Jesus says in John 14:7, 9, "If you really knew me, you would know my Father as well. From now on, you do know him and have seen him . . . Don't you know me, Philip, even after I have been among you such a long time? Anyone who has seen me has seen the Father." Also, Jesus says, "I am the good shepherd. I know my sheep and my sheep know me" (John 10:14). Jesus was a real, flesh-and-blood person who interacted with and developed relationships with other humans. Sometimes, like with Philip, even his closest disciples failed to truly understand him, but Jesus declares that because they see and know him, they see and know God the Father as well. It is through knowing Jesus that we know God.

So, all that "Yahweh" is, Jesus is. Jesus says, "I am the good shepherd." As we read Psalm 23 and John 10, we see several parallels that show that Jesus is the fulfillment of the hope we find in Psalm 23.

Psalm 23

The LORD our shepherd . . .

leads his sheep

"he leads me beside quiet waters"

guides his sheep

"he guides me in paths of righteousness"

takes them to pasture

"he makes me lie down in green pastures"

stays with them

"I will fear no evil, for you are with me"

protects them

"your rod and your staff, they comfort me"

overflows in his care

"you prepare a table before me . . . my cup overflows"

John 10

Jesus as the good shepherd . . .

leads his sheep

"he calls his own sheep by name and leads them out"

guides his sheep

"he goes on ahead of them, and his sheep follow him because they know his voice"

takes them to pasture

"whoever enters through me will be saved. He will come in and go out, and find pasture"

does not abandon them

"the good shepherd lays down his life . . . The hired hand . . . abandons the sheep"

protects them with his life

"I lay down my life for the sheep"

provides life to the full

"I have come that they may have life, and have it to the full"

Is Jesus claiming to be the subject of Psalm 23? Maybe not directly (e.g., "I am the subject of Psalm 23"), but certainly he claims to be the fulfillment of what David writes about in Psalm 23. David knew his God personally as his shepherd. Jesus, in his own words and using the same imagery of Psalm 23, lets us know that he is that very same shepherd that David so skillfully describes. Jesus draws out the reality of how he as our good shepherd cares for and protects us as his sheep. Just as Jesus reminded Philip, we see and know God when we see and know Jesus. As we look at Psalm 23, let's keep in mind that Jesus is our shepherd and our God, who cares for us with an unending love.

Three major themes can be seen in Psalm 23: the Shepherd's provision, the Shepherd's guidance, and the Shepherd's protection.

The Shepherd's Provision

"The Lord is my shepherd, I shall not be in want" (Psalm 23:1).

Here David declares that God is his shepherd. The second statement "I shall not be in want" comes as a simple declaration of trust. As a result of God being his shepherd, David sees no reason to think that God will not provide for him. Just as a shepherd provides for his sheep, David knows that with God as his shepherd, he will be provided for. He will not be "in want."

When Jesus is our shepherd, we have no reason to think that he will not provide for us. Indeed, because he is our shepherd, he will provide for us. He is a faithful and caring Shepherd. We will not be in want. We will lack nothing.

This is easy enough to say, but sometimes it seems that life works differently. We do lack. We don't have perfect, cozy lives. But David isn't saying that he will have all his wants and desires met. He is saying that God as our shepherd provides for us. David is saying more about his own attitude or perspective on life than on how God will provide for him. Just like David, when we approach life from the perspective or attitude that God is our shepherd, then we will begin to see how God is at work to provide for us.

"He makes me lie down in green pastures, he leads me beside quiet waters, he restores my soul" (Psalm 23:2-3a).

Just as any shepherd would seek out places for the sheep to rest and to be refreshed, David's Shepherd provides the same in his life. "Lying down in green pastures" suggests rest and nourishment. "Leading me beside quiet waters" suggests guidance and refreshment. "Restoring my soul" suggests a revitalizing or rejuvenating of the person ("he restores me" or "he restores my strength" are other ways to stay this). David is saying that his own life is filled with peace, rest, and satisfaction because of the presence and guidance of his Shepherd. Because the Shepherd provides peace, rest, and satisfaction, David lacks nothing.

In the same way, our Shepherd's presence and guidance in our lives brings us peace, rest, and satisfaction. Ephesians 2:11-22 emphasizes the peace and sustenance we have because of a relationship with Christ. Hebrews 4:16 says we can approach God with confidence to find grace to help us in our time of need. Philippians 4:4-13 reminds us that God's peace is ours when we keep our trust in him. We find contentment, regardless of how great our need, when we turn to God for strength. Our perspective makes all the difference. Our attitude determines the outcome of our lives. By keeping our focus on our Shepherd, we can find rest and rejuvenation for our lives, no matter how grave our circumstances appear.

The Shepherd's Guidance

In Psalm 23:2-3, the shepherd doesn't just make provisions for the sheep and then expect them to find what he has provided on their own. He doesn't open the gate and send them wandering to find the pastures and streams. Instead, the shepherd guides them to the place of provision.

The guidance the shepherd provides is very necessary for the kind of animal a sheep is. Sheep are not very smart and will go astray, get lost, and get into difficulties if the shepherd is not leading them and keeping them together. Without the shepherd to get them where they need to be, the sheep would not live well. They would miss out on the provision and protection that the shepherd gives.

This is much like our own lives, as David suggests in the Psalm. David says His Shepherd, the Lord, is providing this guidance in his own life. And this is what Jesus does in our lives as well. Without the leading and guiding that Jesus does in our lives, we would be like the sheep who go astray and get into difficulties. Because Jesus guides us, we can find the rest and peace that he provides.

"He guides me in the paths of righteousness for his name's sake." (Psalm 23:3b).

Using the sheep and shepherd metaphor, here David tells us that the shepherd keeps the sheep on the right path. Sheep on the wrong path would stumble into trouble. Sheep on the right paths make it to the rest and peace that the shepherd provides. So our Shepherd Jesus will guide us along the right paths as well.

"Paths of righteousness" reminds us that the paths our lives take have a moral element. In other words, the right paths for us are found when we live in a way that is pleasing and honoring to God. Our lives should be filled with joy, peace, love, patience, kindness, and other qualities rather than being filled with hate, selfishness, pride, and other sinful attitudes and behaviors. Our lives can be filled with what pleases God when we are willingly allowing God to guide our lives because of his presence in our lives (Romans 8:5-10; Galatians 5:16-26).

Rebelling against God through sin is what puts us on the wrong path. And we all do this at times – we go astray like a sheep does. (Isaiah 53:6;

Romans 6:12-13). But it only happens when we, like a sheep, take our focus off our Guide, and we try to make it on our own strength and ability. The Guide who is present in our lives, the one who leads us as we trust him, is the only one who will keep us on the paths of righteousness, the right path, the life that is pleasing to him.

Notice how the verse ends: "for his name's sake." It is the reputation of the shepherd that is at stake when the sheep are following him. Our Shepherd leads us on the righteous path (and provides for us along the way) because it demonstrates that he is the Good Shepherd, not a hired hand who will desert us (John 10:11-13). When we follow him, it brings him honor and his name is held up in high regard by those around us. So when we stick with our Shepherd, others see that we have a Good Shepherd.

But when we drift away and rebel against our Shepherd through sin, it is not a reflection on him but on us. It shows us by our natural and true nature – sinners who need the rescue of the Savior. He is still the Good Shepherd who willingly gave his life for us (John 10:10-11). And we help others see who he is and we bring him honor when we accept his guidance in our lives to take us on the right paths, to take us where our lives should go.

The Shepherd's Protection

"Even though I walk through the valley of the shadow of death, I will fear no evil, for you are with me; your rod and your staff, they comfort me. You prepare a table before me in the presence of my enemies. You anoint my head with oil; my cup overflows"
(Psalm 23:4-5).

Now David turns his attention to the protection the Shepherd provides. In these verses, David continues the shepherd and sheep metaphor (v. 4) but then shifts to a personal metaphor, as if the Lord is his host at a meal (v. 5). Both verses emphasize the protection that comes from a relationship with the Lord.

Just as sheep are safe when they are with their shepherd, even in the darkest and most dangerous places, so David is safe in the worst of circumstances because the Lord is with him. The Lord's presence with him gives him confidence ("I will fear no evil") to face whatever the world throws at him. The shepherd's rod and staff were the tools he used to protect his sheep from attack and to guide his sheep to safety. The protection these provided to the sheep gave reassurance to the sheep that they were safely in the shepherd's care. David feels that same comfort and reassurance as if God has a rod and staff to protect him. Notice that a rod and staff are not tools that protect from a long distance. They are tools that protect when the shepherd is close to his sheep. So David's comfort comes from God's close presence with him and the reassurance that God is actively guiding him and keeping him safe.

David's confidence and comfort are the same attitudes we can have when we reflect on the presence of Jesus in our lives and what his presence means for our protection. Just like David, we can be confident even in the darkest and worst of circumstances because the Lord is with us. His presence in our lives means that we can face whatever the world throws at us with confidence, knowing that he will never leave us or forsake us (Deuteronomy 31:8; Matthew 28:20). And no matter what happens to us, including the worst disasters and the worst pain, we can trust Jesus to always love us and to bring us safely home to be with him forever (Philippians 1:19-26; John 14:1-3; Romans 8:35-38). God's presence in our lives brings us the confidence to face our difficulties and his presence also brings us comfort and reassurance, reminding us that God is actively keeping us safely in his loving hands, no matter what happens (Romans 8:28, 35-38).

"Surely goodness and love will follow me all the days of my life, and I will dwell in the house of the LORD *forever" (Psalm 23:6).*

David closes this Psalm with the confident affirmation that his life is in good hands because his life is in God's hands. David says that goodness and love will follow him for the rest of his life. Where does this goodness and love come from? From God in his life. David expects that his life will be full of God's goodness and love because he trusts God to be with him as his Lord and Shepherd.

"Love" here is a word for grace in the OT – *chesed* – which emphasizes God's devotion or loyal love. "Follow" is the more intensive or aggressive idea of pursuing someone rather than just "following" someone like a pet follows its master (1 Sam. 17:52; 30:8; Ps. 143:3; 34:15; 18:37). It is the idea of keeping after someone until the objective is accomplished. God's goodness and loyal love will relentlessly pursue David his whole life. God is not giving up on him.

David closes the Psalm with the statement "I will dwell in the house of the LORD forever." The idea of dwelling is the idea of residing or returning again and again; it has the idea of ongoing presence or consistency of presence. David's desire to be in the house of the Lord emphasizes his desire to be in God's presence all the time. The word "forever" ("length of days") emphasizes the present and future of David's life. Other places that "length of days" is used also focus on "the rest of one's life" (Deut. 30:20; see Ps. 23:6 in HCSB and NET). So the idea is that David wants to be with the Lord throughout his life. It his way of saying that God's presence in his life is good and that this is what he wants for all of his life. God is relentlessly pursuing David with His goodness and devotion, and David wants to accept God's attention and enjoy God's presence.

As followers of Christ, this is the same desire that we should have. Because Jesus is in our lives and will be with us forever (Matthew 28:20), we can be sure that his goodness and loyal love will fill our lives and that he will bring us safely into the Father's presence. We will be in God's presence forever because we are already in his presence through a relationship with Jesus. We can trust him to be with us and we can have confidence that our lives are secure in God's hands. Because the Lord is our Shepherd, there is consistency and constancy, security and safety, durability and delight, trust and triumph, relationship and rejoicing. Living for God is the place to be.

Close to the Shepherd

As we've studied Psalm 23, the picture of a shepherd and his sheep reminds us about the provision, guidance, and protection that God gives us as he cares for us. The Psalm is not saying that we will never face difficulties and challenges in our lives. It is saying that when we stick close to our Shepherd, we can face anything that life throws at us. We can confidently face life, whether things are going well or not, when we are walking through life with Jesus the Shepherd at our side.

Throughout my life, I have experienced the ups and downs that happen in any relationship, including a relationship with God. There have been times when I've been distracted from my relationship with God, when I've tried to live on my own strength and when I've put myself first instead of putting Christ first in my life. Every Christian who is honest with himself or herself will admit that it is easy to drift away like sheep go astray. But I'm so glad that God does not abandon us at those moments, that God continues to be at work in our lives and to gently nudge us back toward the safe and satisfying place of walking close to him. Sometimes we can be persistent in our wandering and it breaks his heart to see us wandering into the dangers of sin and self-pride. Sometimes he will put challenges in our lives either to wake us up and get us back on the right path or to push us into an even greater and deeper level of following him.

When my son Ethan was just a few weeks old, I feel God gave my wife Christy and me a push toward a deeper level of trusting him on a daily basis. I wouldn't say we had wandered from the path of following him. I just think God was ready for us to walk even closer to him than we ever had.

When Ethan was 6 weeks old, he developed double pneumonia and stopped breathing. Looking back, we can see God's hand in so many things that happened in those moments and the weeks to follow that were God's ways of reminding us to trust him. Ethan stopped breathing at the doctor's office and there were experienced nurses and our doctor there to revive him and keep him alive until the life-support team arrived with the ambulance. The weeks in the hospital as Ethan went through the recovery process were filled with amazing reminders of

God's love, care, and protection. Hundreds and hundreds of people were praying for us, sending us notes of encouragement, or stopping by to support us. Through this experience, we came to accept that God would take care of us and that we could trust him, even if Ethan would have died. We came to the point of being willing to accept God's will in our lives and in Ethan's life, even if it was not what we would have wanted.

The Shepherd's provision, guidance, protection were very clear to us. We were extremely grateful that Ethan lived and recovered completely, but we also found that God's protection is not just about physical safety. His care and protection in our lives is all about being at work in our hearts even in the midst of the worst of life's experiences. "Even though I walk through the valley of the shadow of death, I will fear no evil, for you are with me" (Psalm 23:4). Through this experience, we found that God's goodness and love truly are following us forever and we can trust him completely no matter what life may bring.

So stick close to the Shepherd. Look for hope despite your circumstances. Learn to trust the Good Shepherd no matter what life may bring.

As we learned to trust our Shepherd to care for Ethan's life, Christy's and my life verse became Habakkuk 3:18-19.

"Yet I will rejoice in the LORD, I will be joyful in God my Savior. The Sovereign LORD is my strength; he makes my feet like the feet of a deer, he enables me to go on the heights."

Life can be messy. It can be full of trouble and tough times. Life's circumstances can feel overwhelming. Habakkuk 3:18-19 is not denying that. Just read the rest of Habakkuk to see that Habakkuk took this attitude despite his circumstances. He chose the path of hope no matter what life would bring.

In light of the challenges we all face, here is how I paraphrase Habakkuk 3:18-19 for our own lives:

"Though everything in my life goes completely downhill and life is miserable and appears to have no hope, even so, I will keep rejoicing in the Lord. I'll stick with an attitude of joy that is focused on

God my Savior. This joy is possible only because the Sovereign Lord is my source of strength. As I stick close to him, he enables me and gives me stability so I can walk through life as sure-footed and nimble as a deer that knows how to live in rough country. He enables me to travel through the tough things of my life like a deer can travel in rocky high places without slipping or falling."

The path will not always be easy, but if Jesus is your Shepherd, he will be with you the whole way. Walk with me in trusting and staying close to the Shepherd all the days of your life.

If you have not begun following Jesus as your Shepherd, I invite you to find out why Jesus is the only one who is worthy and able to be our Provider, Guide, and Protector. Not only the quality of your life but your eternal destiny depends on whether you trust Jesus with your life and accept his offer of eternal life, which he made available to us through his death and resurrection (John 6:40; 17:3; Rom. 5:6-11).

Have the confidence and hope that David expressed when he said, "The LORD is my shepherd, I shall not be in want . . ."

www.ingramcontent.com/pod-product-compliance
Ingram Content Group UK Ltd.
Pitfield, Milton Keynes, MK11 3LW, UK
UKHW020215250726
13967UKWH00001B/6